HEADLAND WALKS
ST IVES to SENNEN

Peter Stanier

Safety Notes

This book describes and recommends a few very nice walks to some interesting headlands, suitable for the average visitor to be undertaken in good weather. It is not a walker's manual. However, every year a few folk experience difficulties and it is always wise to give your personal safety some consideration. Although easily accessible this is still a wild coastline and difficulties may arise if you stray from the beaten track.

Please do not try and take pictures from every location that the photographer used in *Headland Walks* as some are off your route, requiring rock climbing experience.

Carry a mobile phone, whistle and a pocket torch. Phone reception is quite good in West Penwith but there are blind spots. If you see or are involved in an accident phone 999 and ask for the Coastguard. Make sure you give your location accurately. A pocket First Aid Kit may also prove useful.

The international distress signal for hills and mountains is: six long flashes of a torch or blasts of a whistle, shouts, waves in succession, repeated at one minute intervals.

Several of the headlands have coastguard stations manned by Coastwatch volunteers and others have houses close by. During daylight hours in the summer there will be plenty of visitors walking on the headlands.

Headland Walks – St Ives to Sennen

© **Peter Stanier**

First Edition published June 2005

Designed and Typeset: Tobi Carver

Photography & Maps: Tobi Carver

Printed & Published by:
The St Ives Printing & Publishing Company,
High Street, St Ives, Cornwall TR26 1RS UK.

www.stivesnews.co.uk

ISBN 0 948385 38 3

FOREWORD

SPECTACULAR WALKS from a SCENIC ROAD

Ancient, almost beyond the memory of man, the north coast road (B3306) winds in an inexplicable manner from St Ives to Land's End. If, on occasion, motorists are tempted to exclaim: "Surely this road was never designed for cars!" they would be right. Winding up hills, down into picturesque villages and along the coastal plain the driver is following the ancient track of cattle herder, wagoner, rider, miner and mule train through a landscape of iron age field systems, still in use today. And, through a post industrial landscape now cherished as nature reclaims it once again.

So amazing is this wonderful road that most visitors are content with the scenic drive, perhaps with a stop atop Rosewall Hill, in Zennor village or at the lay-by near Carn Galver Mine. Fewer venture on the short walks to the headlands below – beyond which is nothing but the wild Atlantic Ocean and America. Those who do are rewarded with some of the most varied, spectacular and accessible cliff-scape in Britain.

Headland Walks arose out of a realisation by Peter Stanier that many visitors to West Penwith were perhaps missing out on visiting some of the headlands simply because they assumed the going might be hard and the headland disappointing. Nothing could be further from the case. While it is true that St Ives Head (the Island) has a tarmac path around it and Bosigran Castle is approached by a stony path, there is nothing described in this little guide that should afford the average visitor any difficulty. At journey's end each headland has its own markedly distinct character on this fantastic coastline.

All the headlands along the cliffs are linked by the Cornwall Coast Path, so longer walks can be entertained simply by, say, taking the walk to Gurnard's Head, then joining the Coast Path to Bosigran Castle giving a good afternoon's walk. But, be careful! For while using this guide to visit a headland is for all, linking the walks is more the province of the serious walker.

Toni Carver

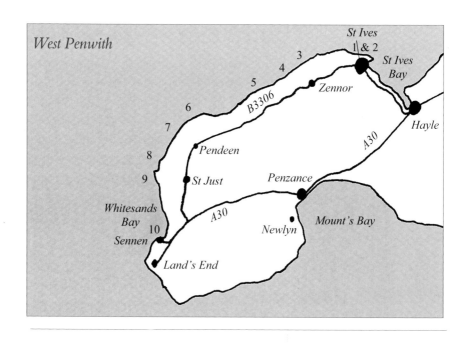

HEADLAND WALKS – ST IVES to SENNEN

Walk 1 – The Island & Porthmeor Beach .... page 9
Walk 2 – Clodgy Point .... page 13
Walk 3 – Zennor Head .... page 15
Walk 4 – Gurnard's Head .... page 19
Walk 5 – Bosigran Castle .... page 23
Walk 6 – Pendeen Watch .... page 27
Walk 7 – Botallack Head & Levant .... page 31
Walk 8 – Kenidjack Castle .... page 35
Walk 9 – Cape Cornwall .... page 37
Walk 10 – Pedn-Men-Du & Mayon Cliff .... page 41

INTRODUCTION

This small book aims to give a selection of easy walks to explore the fantastic coastline between St Ives and Sennen Cove, with the chance of visiting the Land's End itself. Keen walkers, of course, will wish to explore the whole length of this section of the South West Coastal Footpath, a distance of 19 miles (30 kms) which might be accomplished in a very full and tiring day although with little time to stop and explore.

The Penwith Coast provides many exhilarating views

These Headland Walks guide you to places specially chosen for their easy access yet with many points of interest and exhilarating views. The first two walks are accessed on foot from St Ives but the starting points of the rest can be reached first by car or bus via the B3306 coast road between St Ives and St Just, with a last mile along the A30 before turning down to Sennen Cove. In fact, the B3306 is worth travelling on even without stopping for a walk. It is not a fast road, and its picturesque route winds its way over granite moorland hills and between tiny stone-walled fields, hamlets and mining landscapes, all with superb vistas and the sea as a backdrop. But why not stop a moment and enjoy it more?

The walks are intentionally short and easy, but there are many hints of places to visit beyond. Points of geological or historical interest found along the way are also briefly described. Most of the footpaths followed by the walks are well signposted, as is the South West Coastal Footpath which is met everywhere.

TIME for a WALK

The times given are an indication of how long a walk or stroll may take – none is long, but you will probably want to relax and take in the atmosphere, watching the sea, the birds, seals, examine the flora or even watch rock-climbers on the granite cliffs at Bosigran or Sennen. But a warning: keep away from steep cliff edges, mine workings (some shafts are still unfenced!) and remember that sudden waves can unexpectedly wash you off the rocks if you dare scramble down to the water's edge.

The NATIONAL TRUST

It is perhaps of no surprise that much of the coastline is now owned and preserved by the National Trust, including many of the headlands described here. Of added interest the Trust even has a working steam engine in its house perched on the cliff edge at Levant Mine.

GEOLOGY

Although much of the Land's End peninsula is coarse granite, it is exposed at relatively few places along the north coast cliffs. We find other rocks instead, such as the dark igneous greenstone at St Ives, Zennor Head, Gurnard's Head, Botallack and Kenidjack. There are also volcanic rocks as well as metamorphic rocks, which have been altered by heat or pressure, such as killas (slate). Where granite does appear it is of special geological interest when we can see the

Much of the Cornish coastline is owned, managed and maintained by The National Trust

6

contact where it has intruded into the surrounding 'country' rocks such as the killas.

The boldest granite cliff is at Bosigran, but it is found again on the east side of Portheras Cove near Pendeen Watch, at Carn Gloose near Cape Cornwall and the whole coast from Sennen Cove to Land's End and beyond. Many of the cliffs are indented with deep narrow clefts known as 'zawns'.

There are also examples of 'raised beaches', which are exposures of fossilised beach deposits from times when sea level was higher. 'Head' is a deposit of brownish earth and jumbled rock fragments, seen overlying the bedrock at the back of many coves. It was formed as a result of frost-shattering when the area was subjected to permafrost conditions during the Ice Age.

*Situated beside the B3306 St Ives to St Just coast road stand
the two engine houses of Carn Galver mine, a prominent
reminder of the area's industrial heritage*

MINING

There is much evidence for mining of tin and copper all along the coast, from ruined engine houses to abandoned shafts, waste tips and other ruins, with adits (drainage tunnels) exposed in the cliffs. Geevor Mine at Pendeen was the last working tin mine in the district. It finally closed in 1990 but the surface workings are now preserved as a museum and well worth visiting. Not so many years ago, the sea water in the cove below was once discoloured reddish with waste from the mining activities.

*The RMS Mulheim, in 2003, became the latest in a long
history of shipwrecks along Penwith's north coast*

SHIPWRECKS

This coast is harsh and unforgiving to mariners. There have been many ship-wrecks, and most ships falling foul of the rocks have become total losses; only a lucky few stranded and managed to escape. The main causes have been stormy weather, fog or simply poor navigation.

FIELDS ALONG the COAST

A broad coastal platform lies between the cliff tops and the parallel range of rough moorland hills with their rocky granite tors. It is carpeted with a maze of tiny irregular-shaped fields, many of which may date from prehistory. The hedge boundaries were created by the clearance of stones to form the fields. These dry-set granite stone walls often have large stones along the base known as 'grounders', while many blocks too large to move still lie in the grass. The coastal road winds its way along the edge of the hills and through some of these fields.

MAPS

The two Ordnance Survey maps covering the area are the 1: 50 000 Landranger 203 Land's End, with more detail given on the 1: 25 000 scale Explorer 102, Land's End. However, no map is really necessary unless you wish to explore further.

THE ISLAND & PORTHMEOR BEACH

Time: *Not long!*
Access: *Easily, from the town of St Ives, via the Island Car Park at the end of Island Road; there is even wheelchair access to part of the headland.*

THIS is an economy walk for those staying in the heart of St Ives.

The Island, as it is called, is actually a rocky headland. It was once known as Pendinas ('Pedn Enys' or Head Island) and may have been defended as a fort in prehistoric times. Many centuries later the fishing settlement in the Down'long part of St Ives grew up on the low strand between The Island and the mainland.

The headland gives shelter to St Ives harbour and a light was shown here at night for guiding sailors in the 16th century.

The Island is crowned by a chapel, battery and coastguard lookout. The distinctive little St Nicholas' Chapel on the west summit is dedicated to a patron saint of seafarers for whom it also served as a daymark. It was nearly demolished in 1904 by the War Office who had been using it as a store, but fierce public outrage forced them to stop and local shipowning magnate Sir Edward Hain paid for it to be rebuilt in 1911 to commemorate the coronation of King George V.

The chapel was restored again in 1971 through the help of J.F. Holman. This landmark is a focus for walkers and provides fine views over the town, St Ives Bay and the two beaches of Porthmeor and Porthgwidden. Its walls also provide shelter from the wind on stormy days!

St Nicholas' Chapel, in its present state

Victorian gun mountings and emplacements can still be seen on the Island. Behind on the left is the gunner's barracks, while in the distance is St Nicholas' Chapel

The Battery was sited at the east end of The Island, for defending the harbour and Porthmeor Beach from enemy incursions. Three circular gun positions of the Victorian period can be seen close to a building which was the gunners' quarters.

The larger emplacement on the very headland supports the coastguard lookout which is now manned by members of the National Coastwatch Institution. Small fishing boats come out from the harbour to work with hand-lines off the headland where the

tide sweeps in and out of St Ives Bay.

The Island is also a good place for watching seabirds, and gannets are a fantastic sight on stormy days, skim-

A National Coastwatch Institution (NCI) volunteer keeps an eye out over Porthgwidden Beach from the St Ives NCI lookout on the east end of The Island

A view from the coastpath around The Island, looking over the sea, under which lie the remains of the Alba. Beyond are Porthmeor Beach and Barnoon Cemetery, where you will find a memorial to the Alba's crew

ming the waves and plunging for fish. Sea creatures can be spotted at times, such as dolphins, basking sharks, the strange sunfish and even the occasional small whale. Seals are common here and all along the coast.

A dramatic shipwreck still remembered in the town was that of the 3,700-ton Panamanian steamship *Alba* on 31st January 1938. She was carrying Welsh coal from Barry Docks to Citavecchia in Italy and came ashore in heavy weather at the east end of Porthmeor Beach.

In full view of spectators on the shore, the St Ives motor lifeboat *Caroline Parsons* took off her crew but capsized, losing five of the sailors. The *Alba*'s boiler is often visible at low tide at The Island end of Porthmeor Beach, and very occasionally the shifting sand reveals more of the wreck. You will find a memorial to members of the crew in the Barnoon Cemetery which commands the whole bay.

Futher: *Walk on the golden sands of Porthmeor Beach at low tide, or continue out to Man's Head and Clodgy Point (walk 2).*

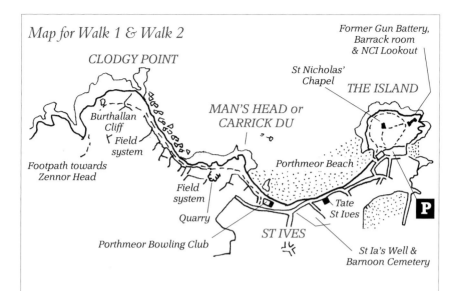

Map for Walk 1 & Walk 2

Former Gun Battery, Barrack room & NCI Lookout

CLODGY POINT

St Nicholas' Chapel

THE ISLAND

Burthallan Cliff

MAN'S HEAD or CARRICK DU

Field system

Footpath towards Zennor Head

Porthmeor Beach

Field system

Quarry

Tate St Ives

ST IVES

P

Porthmeor Bowling Club

St Ia's Well & Barnoon Cemetery

From Walk 1, The Island & Porthmeor Beach, simply climb the steps from the beach to the road. Once on the road walk with your back towards the Island until you reach a car park and toilet block opposite St Ia's Well (one set of steps will take you into the car park). From the car park you will clearly see the Bowling and Putting Greens.

St Nicholas' Chapel, with superb views over St Ives, the sea or the Island itself, offers an opportunity for a spot of relaxation

12

WALK 2

CLODGY POINT

Time: *One hour.*

Access: *Start outside the St Ives Tate Gallery, overlooking Porthmeor Beach. There is wheelchair access as far as Man's Head.*

This walk starts at Porthmeor Beach in St Ives and follows the South West Coastal Footpath out of the town. Facing the sea, turn left (west) and just opposite St Ia's Well, which is tucked in under the wall of Barnoon Cemetery, the coastal footpath passes the bowling and putting greens as it leaves the town.

The path is well made as far as Man's Head or Carrick Du at the far end of the beach. There are good views from here, over the popular surfing beach where a great expanse of golden sand is exposed at low tide. Across on the far side you will see the unmistakable shape of The Island. There is an old greenstone quarry at Carrick Du, worked for roadstone from the late 19th century. Old mine shafts and traces of engine houses in the undergrowth belonged to the Carrick Du Mine, which worked for cop-

Man's Head, or Carrick Du (Black Rock), looking towards The Island

13

Burthallan Cliff, Clodgy Point, looking up towards the distinctive rock outcrop which is clearly visible from St Ives

per in the first half of the 19th century just west of the headland.

Although slightly rougher, there is still an easy path continuing along the edge of a low cliff above a bouldered shore to Burthallan Cliff, on the end of which are the low rocks of Clodgy Point. On the slopes here you can detect the low banks of old field boundaries.

This simple walk allows you to quickly escape the bustle of St Ives, and find somewhere to sit alone by the cliffs and the sea. Clodgy is not a high headland, but there are enticing views of a rugged coastline and three headlands to the west: Hor Point, Pen Enys Point and Carn Naun Point.

Further: *The coast path suddenly becomes steeper and more difficult but the temptation is to follow it to just one more point, and then another! Certainly, Hor Point and Pen Enys Point near Trevalgan are within reach. The American steamer* Bessemer City, *5686 tons, was wrecked under Pen Enys Point in 1936 and in the following June fog brought the Italian* Aida Lauro, *4538 tons, onto the rocks in the same spot.*

Even further: *Beyond here the walk follows one of the remotest stretches of coast all the way to Zennor Head (walk 3), not far on the map but a strenuous outing. Once the village of Zennor is gained, a footpath can be followed through the fields back to St Ives.*

WALK 3
ZENNOR HEAD

Time: *One hour.*

Access: *Start in Zennor, a delightful small granite village with a church set among tiny fields between the coast and moorland hills, just off the B3306 coast road, 5 miles from St Ives. There is a small car park.*

A narrow lane between the church and the Tinners Arms bends behind the pub and eventually becomes a path which leads out to Zennor Head.

The headland, which was given to the National Trust in 1954, provides views up and down the coast. It consists of slates and greenstone, while the hills close inland are solid granite. This untamed landscape is a great place to be in the evening. The highest point is 315 feet (96 metres) and the headland slopes steeply down to the sea towards the north.

Small mine workings and shafts across the headland, much overgrown, were probably part of the Zennor Head Mine which worked before the mid-19th century. Lonely Tregerthen Cliff is viewed to the east, where the Coastal Footpath follows a wild coast as far as St Ives. On the west side, the steepest cliffs of the headland overlook a zawn and a narrow ridge known as the Horse's Back. This in turn overlooks Pendour Cove, the place to which the mermaid of the legend enticed Zennor chorister Matthew Trewhella.

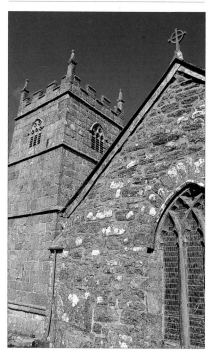

Zennor Church, one of Cornwall's prettiest churches

Walkers, enjoying the early spring sunshine, approach Zennor Head itself

Make a day of it when you return to Zennor. The remarkable granite church, dedicated to St Senara, has the famous wooden bench-end carved with the mermaid who is the source of the local legend. Outside is a memorial to John Davey of Boswednack, who died in 1891 and was said to be the last to speak Cornish. There is also the Zennor Wayside Folk Museum, with its fascinating collection of all sorts of Cornish items. Refreshments after all this can be found in the Tinners Arms.

Two early 20th century writers are associated with Zennor. In 1906-7, the naturalist W.H. Hudson overwintered in a cottage here, and he described his experiences in his book *The Land's End*. D.H. Lawrence and his German wife Frieda lived at Zennor from March 1916 until July 1917, first staying at the Tinners Arms and later renting cottages at nearby Higher Tregerthen where Lawrence completed writing *Women in Love*. Their stay was marred by the suspicious authorities (there were even rumours of secret signalling with German U-boats creeping offshore) and the Lawrences were suddenly given three days' notice to leave Cornwall. Lawrence had found contentment

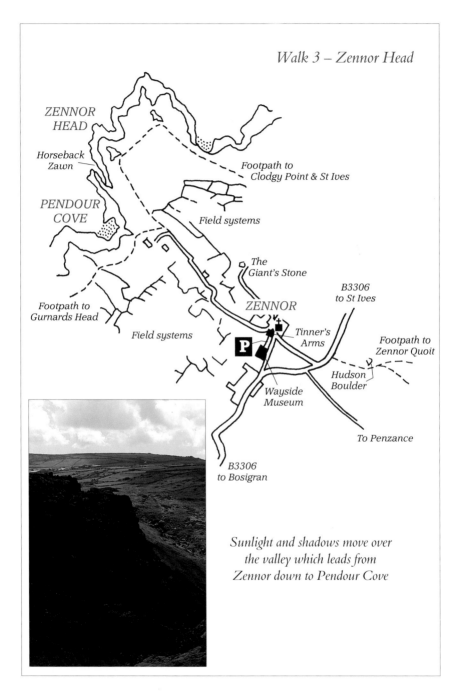

Walk 3 – Zennor Head

ZENNOR HEAD

Horseback Zawn

Footpath to Clodgy Point & St Ives

PENDOUR COVE

Field systems

The Giant's Stone

B3306 to St Ives

Footpath to Gurnards Head

ZENNOR

Field systems

P

Tinner's Arms

Footpath to Zennor Quoit

Hudson Boulder

Wayside Museum

To Penzance

B3306 to Bosigran

Sunlight and shadows move over the valley which leads from Zennor down to Pendour Cove

Zennor's Wayside Museum provides a wonderful diversion for those visiting Zennor. The building, with its distinctive waterwheel houses a collection covering the history of the village and its inhabitants

here and he wrote of Zennor: 'It is a most beautiful place, a tiny village nestling under high, shaggy moorhills, a big sweep of sea beyond. It is the best place I have been in.'

Further: *Climb up on Zennor Hill and seek out the curiously shaped granite rocks which include a logan stone (a perched one which moves). A large granite block on the northern slope, overlooking Zennor village, the Head and the coast, has been carved 'W.H. HUDSON OFTEN CAME HERE'.*

Looking along the path up the valley towards Zennor Hill

18

WALK 4
GURNARD'S HEAD

Time: *One hour.*

Access: *Start at Treen about 2 miles west of Zennor on the B3306 coast road, where the Gurnard's Head Hotel is an obvious landmark.*

A lane to the right of the pub passes the old coastguard cottages in the hamlet of Treen. Follow this to find the footpath through the fields, then across the Coastal Footpath before descending to the long rocky headland. Gurnard's Head is so named because its shape has a close likeness to that of the fish's head. It is also known as Trereen Dinas, for it is the site of a 'cliff castle,' a type of prehistoric promontory fort common in Cornwall.

There are traces of three defensive ramparts cutting across the neck of land connected to the mainland, which is the weakest point since steep cliffs provide protection around the rest of the site. Inside, at least 18 platforms for round houses have been traced in two areas on the more sheltered east slope. The site was excavated in 1939 and its occu-pation dated to the second century BC in the Iron Age.

The dark cliffs of the west face of Gurnard's Head are the fiercest. Most of the rocks which form the craggy summits are either volcanic greenstone or pillow lavas, but there are also slates here. A coastguard lookout was established out on the rocky end, which provides an extensive view up and down the coast and out to sea. It was a most lonely spot out of sight of civilization but connected by a telegraph wire on poles.

The remains of Chapel Jane, nestled amongst undergrowth on the cliff edge

There have been many shipwrecks at Gurnard's Head, such as the three-masted barque *Alexander Yeates* which was wrecked in a south-westerly gale under the east side in September 1896. Her crew were rescued by breeches buoy, the same method employed to save the crew of the 299-ton German coaster *Traute Sarnow* wrecked in fog in July 1954 on passage from Cardiff to Ostende with a cargo of anthracite.

Return to the mainland and turn left (east) to follow the Coastal Footpath past the remains of Chapel Jane above Treen Cove to a ruined engine house which was for the Gurnard's Head Mine. Operations had begun before 1821 as the Treen Copper Mine, with a shaft right down on the rocks so close to the sea that it was protected by a stone wall. Below the engine house there was once a seine pilchard fishing station at Lean Point. Beyond Boswednack Cliff can be seen the old count house (office) of Carnelloe Mine on the cliff top, and beyond that Zennor Head. Return to Treen across the fields by another footpath.

Craggy summits of volcanic greenstone and pillow lava provide for some dramatic views at Gurnard's Head

20

The picturesque ruins of the Gurnard's Head mine engine house

Further: *Join the Coastal Footpath to walk eastwards past Boswednack Cliff and Porthglaze Cove to the site of Carnelloe Mine. This was at work in 1862 when two large waterwheels in the cliffside were used for winding from the shafts and working stamps for crushing the ores until the mine closed in 1876. Several shafts were sunk, one very close to the sea. The mineral lodes were a continuation of those worked by the Gurnard's Head Mine.*

Alternatively, walk the Coastal Footpath to the west along Treen Cliff, which provides a good view of the west side of Gurnard's Head. The cliffs continue past Zawn Duel (the devil's zawn) and Carn Gloose to Porthmeor Cove, a place where the junction between the granite and killas (slates) can be seen, with veins of granite cutting through the country rock.

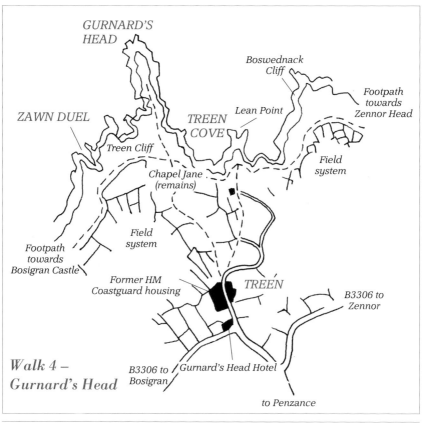

GURNARD'S
HEAD

Boswednack
Cliff

Footpath
towards
Zennor Head

ZAWN DUEL

Lean Point

TREEN
COVE

Treen Cliff

Field
system

Chapel Jane
(remains)

Field
system

Footpath
towards
Bosigran Castle

Field
system

Former HM
Coastguard housing

TREEN

B3306 to
Zennor

Walk 4 –
Gurnard's Head

B3306 to
Bosigran

Gurnard's Head Hotel

to Penzance

*Gurnard's Head, from
the ruins of the
Gurnard's Head mine
engine house.*

WALK 5
BOSIGRAN CASTLE

Time: *One hour.*

Access: *Bosigran is 3 miles by the coast road from Zennor and just over a mile from Treen. The walk starts at a small car park beside the two ruined engine houses, which cannot be missed next to the road. The granite headland was acquired by the National Trust in 1978.*

The pumping engine house of Carn Galver Mine retains its brick-topped chimney but is more ruinous than the winding engine house which faces away from the shaft. This mine produced very little tin when last worked in the 1870s. Its shaft is 780 feet (238 metres) deep. The old count house (office) nearby is now a climbing hut of the Climbers' Club.

Footpaths lead down the shallow valley towards the coast, through small fields bounded by dry-stone walls, perhaps prehistoric in origin. At the bottom of the valley, the stream cascades over the cliff into Porthmoina Cove. Just above are the ruins of a building, an early 19th-century tin dressing works

powered by a waterwheel where ore was stamped (crushed) and 'dressed' to recover the tin mineral cassiterite.

A climbers' path continues down to the main cliff face, but turn right to climb onto the top of the Bosigran Castle, which is 333 feet (101 metres) high and encircled on the landward side by traces of a stone

One of Carn Galver Mine's engine houses

rampart. Among the rocks, gorse and heather of the interior, seek out the 'logan stone'. It is not very large but it can be rocked if you jump up and down at the correct end.

Looking over the gorse bushes towards the summit of Bosigran Castle

A careful descent to the east brings you to the charming and secluded Haldrine Cove; there is no beach here, just granite cliffs.

The large Porthmoina Cove is only accessible to rock climbers, but can be seen from the top of Bosigran Castle and the Coastal Footpath. It has large rounded boulders at the back and can be sandy on occasions according to the movement of currents and storms. Porthmoina Island is a knife edge of rock beneath the impressive granite face of Bosigran Cliff, where climbers can be seen tackling some of the finest granite in the kingdom.

Before returning to the road, it is worth crossing the stream by the old tin mill and following the Coastal Footpath for a little way to the west. It gives a fine view of the Bosigran cliff, and it also passes the top of Commando Ridge, a fantastic arête with pinnacles ascending from the sea. It was used for training men of the commando cliff assault wing in the 1940s and '50s, and there is a commemorative plaque set in the face near the top of the ridge.

The Logan Stone close to the highest point of Bosigran Castle

Further: *To the west, the Rosemergy Cliffs (National Trust) have ridges, pinnacles and zawns. This is wild country – look out for the goats! The cliffs beyond are remote and there are mine shafts and other signs of mining before reaching Morvah.*

Further explorations can be made from the car park back at the road. Up behind are the two viewpoint summits of Carn Galver (816 feet or 249 metres) and Watch Croft (826 feet or 252 metres), both wild areas with granite rocks forming a veritable barrier between the coastal plain and the high moorland interior.

Porthmoina Island

25

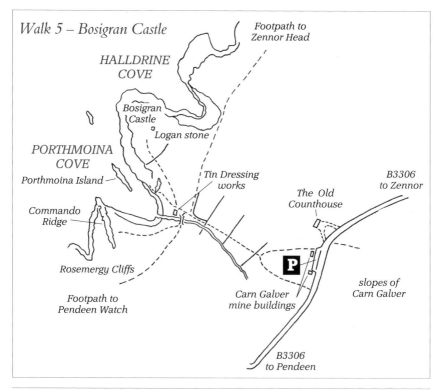

'Commando Ridge' silhouetted against the sea by the evening sun

WALK 6
PENDEEN WATCH

Time: *Not long.*

Access: *The approach is signposted from the B3306 at Higher Boscaswell, where a lane leads for about a mile down to the lighthouse at Pendeen Watch.*

The lighthouse was a relatively late one, built to protect shipping on this hazardous and previously unlit coast between the Longships and Godrevy lighthouses. Offshore is a reef called The Wra or Three Oar Stone.

On stormy days it is easy to see why there was a need for Pendeen Watch lighthouse

The lighthouse was prompted by a series of disastrous shipwrecks and there were even two while it was under construction. The first light was shown in September 1900 and was converted to electricity in 1926.

The keepers' houses, which were built with flat roofs to collect rain water, have been converted to holiday accommodation. The lighthouse has been fully automated since 1995 but is open for visits during the summer months.

The light has a range of 16 sea miles and gives four white flashes every 15 seconds. The fog horn emits a loud blast once every 20 seconds. A white mark was once painted on the cliffs at Bosigran 2 ½ miles along the coast, so the keepers could gauge the visibility and therefore when to turn on the fog signal.

It is said that the light of Trevose Lighthouse further up the Cornish coast is only visible at low tide when viewed from Pendeen Watch; high tide is enough to hide it from view because of the curvature of the earth.

Although not the tallest in the area, Pendeen Watch's lighthouse and its accompanying buildings, is certainly one of the more complex

'The fog horn emits a loud blast every 20 seconds.' Not a good place to stand!

Looking across to the beach of Portheras Cove from the fishermen's sheds between Pendeen Watch and the cove

An easy walk leads down to a small fishing place at Portheras Cove, immediately to the east. This is a delightful cove and the granite cliffs of Carn Clough stand out on the far side of the sandy beach. In September 1963 the 454-ton coaster *Alacrity* was wrecked in Portheras Cove. Belonging to the once famil- iar coaster fleet of F.T. Everard & Sons, she was carrying anthracite from Swansea to Brussels, but all attempts to refloat her failed. Parts of the ship sometimes emerge from the sand at low tides.

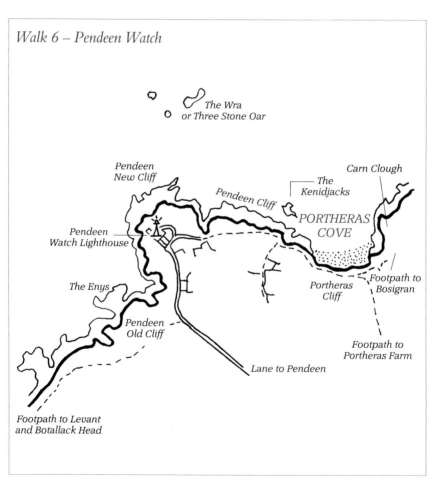

Walk 6 – Pendeen Watch

The Wra
or Three Stone Oar

Pendeen
New Cliff

Carn Clough

The
Kenidjacks

Pendeen Cliff

Pendeen
Watch Lighthouse

PORTHERAS
COVE

The Enys

Portheras
Cliff

Footpath to
Bosigran

Pendeen
Old Cliff

Footpath to
Portheras Farm

Lane to Pendeen

Footpath to Levant
and Botallack Head

BOTALLACK HEAD & LEVANT

Time: *One hour (two hours including Levant visit).*

Access: *From Botallack village, which is just off the B3306 half-way between Pendeen and St Just. Past the Queen's Arms, the lane becomes a rough track leading out to the old Botallack Mine's Count House (now a National Trust information centre) and the headland.*

Alternative access: *Almost opposite the Trewellard Arms in Pendeen, a lane leads down to Levant Mine (National Trust), and Botallack can be approached from there.*

Evidence of the activity of 1907-14, arsenic calciner, flues & chimney

This is a mining landscape and Botallack Head is best known for the twin engine houses of the Crowns section of Botallack Mine, perched on a shelf down the cliffs almost at sea level. The lower house was built in about 1835 to contain a beam engine for pumping to drain the mine, and space was so tight that the chimney stack was incorporated inside the building.

The other house had a winding engine in 1862 to work the inclined Diagonal Shaft which ran out under the sea to a depth of 1,360 feet (414 metres). On stormy days the miners could hear large boulders being rolled about on the sea floor above their heads.

It is not surprising that this dramatic site has been well recorded over the years in sketches, photographs, postcards and calendars. The author Wilkie Collins wrote a terrifying account of his descent in 1850, but royalty also came here, including Victoria and Albert in 1846 and the Duke and Duchess of Cornwall (the future King Edward VII and Queen Alexandra) in 1865.

An inclined timber bridge ran down to the shaft opening, which can still be seen in the rocky cliff close to the sea. At that date there were 11 steam engines at work on the mine which was employing 500 persons above and below ground.

Having closed at the end of the century, Botallack was reworked in 1907-14, when dressing floors, an arsenic calciner, flues and chimney stack were built on the top of the cliff not far from the Count House. There was more activity in the early 1980s when tin prospectors erected a steel headframe over Allen's Shaft.

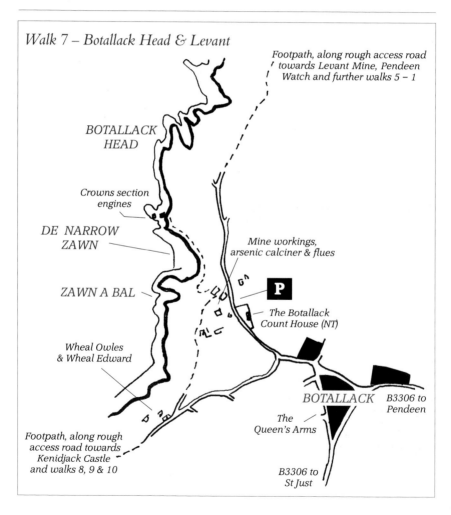

Walk 7 – Botallack Head & Levant

Footpath, along rough access road towards Levant Mine, Pendeen Watch and further walks 5 – 1

BOTALLACK HEAD

Crowns section engines

DE NARROW ZAWN

Mine workings, arsenic calciner & flues

ZAWN A BAL

P

The Botallack Count House (NT)

Wheal Owles & Wheal Edward

BOTALLACK   B3306 to Pendeen

The Queen's Arms

Footpath, along rough access road towards Kenidjack Castle and walks 8, 9 & 10

B3306 to St Just

*The famous and much photographed twin engine houses of the Crowns section
of Botallack Mine, seen here from less familiar viewpoints*

Further: *A walk north-eastwards along the cliff top leads to Levant Mine, which ran out over a mile beneath the sea, with workings at a depth of over 2,100 feet (640 metres). Mining for copper began here in about 1820, and continued until 1910 making this Cornwall's last copper mine. However, tin became increasingly important after 1852.*

A disaster occurred in 1919 when the 'man-engine' lift broke and killed 31 miners, with many others injured. Levant closed in 1930. The site is now owned by the National Trust. A small steam winding engine built in 1840 by Harveys of Hayle has been restored by members of the Trevithick Society and can be seen working during the summer months inside its house on the edge of the cliff at Skip Shaft.

Botallack's last period of activity saw the erection of a headframe over Allen's Shaft

The empty engine house next to it contained a pumping engine. Levant also has a tall chimney stack above the ruined compressor house of 1901, there are traces of the ill-fated man-engine house and its shaft, and there are two old circular powder magazines on the cliffs.

Levant Mine (NT) looking down the coast towards Pendeen Watch

34

WALK 8
KENIDJACK CASTLE

Time: *One hour.*

Access: *As for Botallack, but after passing the Count House turn left (west) along the Coastal Footpath. Abandoned engine houses on the cliff top belonged to West Wheal Owles and Wheal Edward, a tin and copper mine which also ran under the sea. Uranium and pitchblende were mined here too, but mining was abandoned in 1893 after 20 miners were drowned when old flooded workings were broken into.*

Kedinjack Castle is approached on the level from the east. It seems to have been an Iron Age cliff castle, defended by natural rock outcrops and ditches and banks across the neck between North and South Zawn. Hut circles have been identified inside.

The headland of Kenidjack Castle provides wonderful sea views and an incredible peaceful place to pause and relax

Ruinous mine buildings, reclaimed by nature

A quarry was opened on the south side of Kenidjack Castle in the late 19th century and there were attempts to ship off the stone from the cove below. The Cunard steamship *Malta* was wrecked below Kenidjack in October 1889 when on passage from Liverpool to Genoa. This 2244-ton steamship with a brig rig ran onto the rocks in a fog and broke up soon afterwards. Everyone on board was rescued. Kenidjack Castle provides a good view of Cape Cornwall (walk 9).

Further: *To the south of Kenidjack Castle a steep path descends into the narrow Kenidjack or Nancherrow valley which meets the coast in the bay known as*

Porth Ledden. It is crammed with ruins and relics dating from the days of mining. Right down by the sea is a massive stone wheelpit which contained a waterwheel 52 feet (15.8 metres) in diameter. It was connected to drainage pumps in the 1860s, but 30 years before, the valley had the largest waterwheel in Cornwall, at 65 feet (19.8 metres) diameter. There are traces of watercourses everywhere, once serving tin stamping mills and dressing floors, but the most prominent ruin is that of an arsenic works, with remains of flues and a chimney stack.

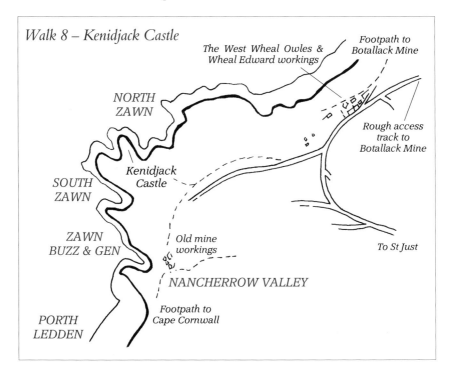

Walk 8 – Kenidjack Castle

The West Wheal Owles & Wheal Edward workings

Footpath to Botallack Mine

NORTH ZAWN

Rough access track to Botallack Mine

Kenidjack Castle

SOUTH ZAWN

ZAWN BUZZ & GEN

Old mine workings

To St Just

NANCHERROW VALLEY

Footpath to Cape Cornwall

PORTH LEDDEN

CAPE CORNWALL

Time: *Under an hour.*

Access: *There is a signposted lane from the centre of St Just village. The lane from St Just leads to a car park almost down to the little landing place on the south side known as Priest's Cove.*

This is the only 'cape' in England, and Cornwall has it! Some even say this should be the true Land's End. The summit of the

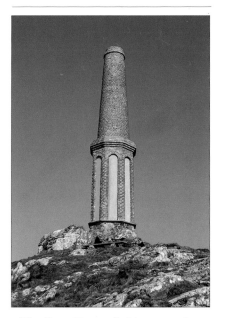

The Cape Cornwall chimney stack, a reminder of the most westerly working mine in England

pyramidal cape is mounted by a rather fancy brick chimney stack of the Cape Cornwall Mine, which was the most westerly in England. It was built for a steam winding engine lower down on the south side, but it created too much draught!

The mine last worked for tin in about 1873 and the old boiler house and the count house have since been converted to dwellings. St Just United was another mine which worked beneath the sea and there are ruins and adits (drainage tunnels) in the cliff on the south side of Priest's Cove. The rock is mostly killas slate.

The view from Cape Cornwall stretches south past the granite cliff of Carn Gloose to Whitesand Bay, Sennen Cove and Land's End. Offshore, the island rocks are called The Brisons. On the other side of the cape, Kenidjack Castle (walk 8) is seen not far away across the waters of Porth Ledden. The ruin of the little chapel of St Helen overlooks this bay from the neck of Cape Cornwall.

The Cape Cornwall NCI station keeps a lookout over The Brisons and out to sea

Nestled on the neck of Cape Cornwall overlooking Porth Ledden lies the ruin of St Helen's Chapel

Further: *Climb the Coastal Footpath to the south, to find the Ballowall Barrow, a chambered cairn which became buried under mine tips. Part has been rebuilt but it is not easy to interpret, having several small chambers built over a period of time. This is a superb place for a burial site, high on Carn Gloose overlooking the Atlantic. The coast path turns inland before descending into the deep Cot Valley, down which a lane leads to the sea at Porth Nanven. There is evidence of mining activity all around (the last was in the 1940s), but the little cove is noted for its round granite boulders on the shore, while the cliff behind exposes a notable example of a 'raised beach' of large rounded pebbles overlain by more angular 'head' material of Ice Age times.*

The former Cape Cornwall Mine Counthouse and Boiler House lay in the shadow of the short lived chimney stack which dominates the skyline of the cape itself

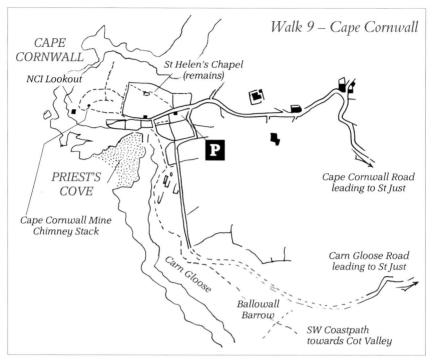

Walk 9 – Cape Cornwall

CAPE CORNWALL

NCI Lookout

St Helen's Chapel (remains)

P

PRIEST'S COVE

Cape Cornwall Mine Chimney Stack

Cape Cornwall Road leading to St Just

Carn Gloose

Carn Gloose Road leading to St Just

Ballowall Barrow

SW Coastpath towards Cot Valley

Fishing boats at rest on the slipway at Priest's Cove

WALK 10
PEDN-MEN-DU AND MAYON CLIFF

Time: *Less than one hour.*

Access: *Start from the car park at the west end of Sennen Cove village near the lifeboat station. Sennen Cove also features the fine surfing beach of Whitesand Bay, teashops and the Old Success Inn.*

A lifeboat was established here in 1853 but it could not always be launched, so a pier was built in 1908 to protect the launch slip. Note also the round capstan house, once used for hauling boats up the small beach between the pier and lifeboat house.

From here follow the Coastal Footpath towards Land's End. It climbs steeply at first, to reach the top of the coarse granite cliffs of Pedn-men-du, much favoured by

Fishing boats lie on the steep slipway beside the Sennen RNLI station

rock climbers. From the coastguard lookout you get the first glimpse of the Land's End cliffs, with the Longships Lighthouse on the rocks a mile offshore. Just along here a tall pinnacle down by the sea is called the Irish Lady Rock.

The story goes that when a lady

The coastpath leading towards the coastguard lookout

fleeing persecution in Ireland was shipwrecked she was seen clinging to this rock for many hours before being swept off and drowned. Her ghost is said to still haunt the rock.

Sennen's much photographed Round House

conclusion that this 'cliff castle' site may date from around 300 BC.

A modern shipwreck caused much interest in the press and attracted visiting spectators after the

Maen Cliff Castle's ancient ramparts, where the South West Coastpath cuts through them

Beyond here is Mayon Cliff (National Trust) and a little headland known as Maen Castle which is enclosed by a small stone rampart. Excavations took place in 1939, with the

Irish Lady rock

A year after its stranding the RMS Mulheim *lies in the cove below Maen Castle battered and torn by the Atlantic waves*

RMS Mulheim ran ashore almost stern-first in Castle Zawn in the early hours of 22nd March 2003. A helicopter rescued the crew while the Sennen Cove lifeboat and Land's End cliff rescue team stood by.

The ship was carrying 2,200 tonnes of shredded motor car plastic from Cork to Lubeck, and once the hull was holed some of this scrap material was soon washing up on the beach at Sennen and fouling fishermen's nets in the area.

A salvage operation, hampered by intermittent bad weather, removed most of the cargo. The ship broke in two a few months later and was left to the forces of the sea.

Further: *It is tempting to continue along the path the short distance to Land's End, but be prepared to have your solitude disturbed by the crowds who approach in great numbers from the main car park there.*

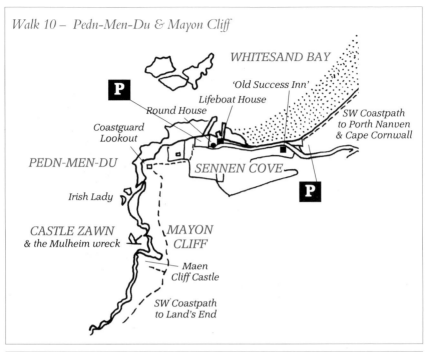

Walk 10 – Pedn-Men-Du & Mayon Cliff

WHITESAND BAY

P

'Old Success Inn'

Lifeboat House

Round House

Coastguard
Lookout

SW Coastpath
to Porth Nanven
& Cape Cornwall

PEDN-MEN-DU

SENNEN COVE

Irish Lady

P

CASTLE ZAWN
& the Mulheim wreck

MAYON
CLIFF

Maen
Cliff Castle

SW Coastpath
to Land's End

Fishing nets and floats hang drying in the spring sunshine below the Round House